Step-by-Step
PROBLEM SOLVING

Grade 5

Frank Schaffer
An imprint of Carson-Dellosa Publishing LLC
Greensboro, North Carolina

Credits

Content Editors: Christine Schwab and Heather Stephan
Copy Editor: Donna H. Walkush
Layout and Cover Design: Lori Jackson

 This book has been correlated to state, common core state, national, and Canadian provincial standards. Visit *www.carsondellosa.com* to search for and view its correlations to your standards.

Copyright © 2012, SAP Group Pte Ltd

Frank Schaffer
An imprint of Carson-Dellosa Publishing LLC
PO Box 35665
Greensboro, NC 27425 USA
www.carsondellosa.com

ISBN 978-1-60996-480-1
01-335111151

Introduction

The **Step-by-Step Problem Solving** series focuses on the underlying processes and strategies essential to problem solving. Each book introduces various skill sets and builds upon them as the level increases. The six-book series covers the following thinking skills and heuristics:

Thinking Skills
- Analyzing Parts and Wholes
- Comparing
- Classifying
- Identifying Patterns and Relationships
- Deduction
- Induction
- Spatial Visualization

Heuristics
- Act It Out
- Draw a Diagram/Model
- Look for a Pattern
- Work Backward
- Make a List/Table
- Guess and Check
- Before and After
- Make Suppositions
- Use Equations

Students who are keen to develop their problem-solving abilities will learn quickly how to:
- make sense of the problem: what am I asked to find?
- make use of given information: what do I know?
- think of possible strategies: have I come across similar problems before?
- choose the correct strategy: apply what I know confidently.
- solve the problem: work out the steps.
- check the answer: is the solution logical and reasonable?

Practice questions follow each skill-set example, and three graded, mixed practices (easy, intermediate, challenging) are provided for an overall assessment of the skills learned. The worked solutions show the application of the strategies used. Students will find this series invaluable in helping them understand and master problem-solving skills.

Table of Contents

Strategy Summary

The following summary provides examples of the various skill sets taught in Step-by-Step Problem Solving.

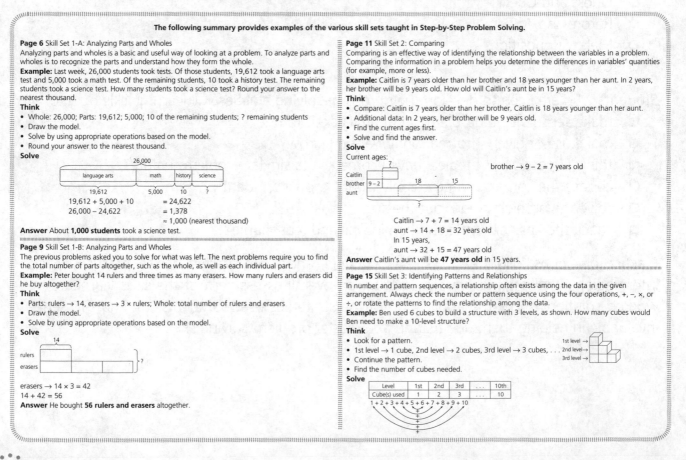

Page 6 Skill Set 1-A: Analyzing Parts and Wholes

Analyzing parts and wholes is a basic and useful way of looking at a problem. To analyze parts and wholes is to recognize the parts and understand how they form the whole.

Example: Last week, 26,000 students took tests. Of those students, 19,612 took a language arts test and 5,000 took a math test. Of the remaining students, 10 took a history test. The remaining students took a science test. How many students took a science test? Round your answer to the nearest thousand.

Think
- Whole: 26,000; Parts: 19,612; 5,000; 10 of the remaining students; ? remaining students
- Draw the model.
- Solve by using appropriate operations based on the model.
- Round your answer to the nearest thousand.

Solve

	26,000		
language arts	math	history	science
19,612	5,000	10	?

$$19,612 + 5,000 + 10 = 24,622$$
$$26,000 - 24,622 = 1,378$$
$$\approx 1,000 \text{ (nearest thousand)}$$

Answer About **1,000 students** took a science test.

Page 9 Skill Set 1-B: Analyzing Parts and Wholes

The previous problems asked you to solve for what was left. The next problems require you to find the total number of parts altogether, such as the whole, as well as each individual part.

Example: Peter bought 14 rulers and three times as many erasers. How many rulers and erasers did he buy altogether?

Think
- Parts: rulers → 14, erasers → 3 × rulers; Whole: total number of rulers and erasers
- Draw the model.
- Solve by using appropriate operations based on the model.

Solve

erasers → 14 × 3 = 42
14 + 42 = 56

Answer He bought **56 rulers and erasers** altogether.

Page 11 Skill Set 2: Comparing

Comparing is an effective way of identifying the relationship between the variables in a problem. Comparing the information in a problem helps you determine the differences in variables' quantities (for example, more or less).

Example: Caitlin is 7 years older than her brother and 18 years younger than her aunt. In 2 years, her brother will be 9 years old. How old will Caitlin's aunt be in 15 years?

Think
- Compare: Caitlin is 7 years older than her brother. Caitlin is 18 years younger than her aunt.
- Additional data: In 2 years, her brother will be 9 years old.
- Find the current ages first.
- Solve and find the answer.

Solve
Current ages:

brother → 9 – 2 = 7 years old

Caitlin → 7 + 7 = 14 years old
aunt → 14 + 18 = 32 years old
In 15 years,
aunt → 32 + 15 = 47 years old

Answer Caitlin's aunt will be **47 years old** in 15 years.

Page 15 Skill Set 3: Identifying Patterns and Relationships

In number and pattern sequences, a relationship often exists among the data in the given arrangement. Always check the number or pattern sequence using the four operations, +, –, ×, or ÷, or rotate the patterns to find the relationship among the data.

Example: Ben used 6 cubes to build a structure with 3 levels, as shown. How many cubes would Ben need to make a 10-level structure?

Think
- Look for a pattern.
- 1st level → 1 cube, 2nd level → 2 cubes, 3rd level → 3 cubes, . . .
- Continue the pattern.
- Find the number of cubes needed.

Solve

Level	1st	2nd	3rd	. . .	10th
Cube(s) used	1	2	3	. . .	10

1 + 2 + 3 + 4 + 5 + 6 + 7 + 8 + 9 + 10

Strategy Summary

$1 + 10 = 11$
5 pairs of $11 \rightarrow 5 \times 11 = 55$
Answer Ben would need 55 cubes to make a 10-level structure.

Page 19 Skill Set 4-A: Deduction
Deduction is a higher-order thinking skill that requires you to infer repeated computations from a given generalization. The information derived from the generalization will lead to a specific answer.
Example: Study the figures. Fill in the table.

Figure	Pattern	Number of Circles
1		
2	1 + 2	3
3		
4		
⋮		
10		

Figure 1   Figure 2   Figure 3

Think
• Study the given information.
• Deduce the pattern from the given information and fill in the numbers.

Answer

Figure	Pattern	Number of Circles
1	1	1
2	1 + 2	3
3	1 + 2 + 3	6
4	1 + 2 + 3 + 4	10
⋮	⋮	⋮
10	1 + 2 + 3 + 4 + 5 + 6 + 7 + 8 + 9 + 10	55

Page 23 Skill Set 4-B: Deduction
Besides applying deduction to shapes and figures, you can also use it to solve for missing numbers or representative letters and symbols in a grid.
Example: Study the number grid. Find the value of the star.
Think
• Study the given information.
• Deduce a pattern from the given information and find the value of the star.

1	2	3
13	*	5
21	34	55

Solve

1	→	2	→	3
13	←	*	←	5
21	→	34	→	55

$1 + 2 = 3$
$2 + 3 = 5$
$3 + 5 = \mathbf{8}$
$5 + \mathbf{8} = 13$
$\mathbf{8} + 13 = 21$
$13 + 21 = 34$
$21 + 34 = 55$

Answer The value of the star is **8**.

Page 26 Skill Set 5: Work Backward
Working backward is a strategy that uses a problem's final answer to find what the problem begins with. Very often, you can trace back the steps and reverse the operations to find the answers.
Example: Think of a number. Double it. Add 8 to the result to get 22. What is the original number?
Think
• Final answer: 22
• Reverse the operations to find the answer.
Solve

| 7 | →(×2)(÷2)→ | 14 | →(+8)(−8)→ | 22 |

reverse operations

$22 − 8 = 14$
$14 ÷ 2 = 7$
Answer The original number is **7**.

Page 30 Skill Set 6-A: Draw a Diagram/Model
Drawing diagrams or models helps you organize the data and identify the relationship among the data found in a problem. This skill set is similar to Analyzing Parts and Wholes, but it involves drawing a different type of model. Here, we will explore problem solving using multiplication and division models.
Example: A farmer had 2,654 hens. He sold 456 hens in 4 days. If an equal number of hens were sold each day, how many days later would the farmer be left with 32 hens?

Think
• Use all of the given data to form the model.
• Work out the appropriate operations.
Solve

Day 1, Day 2, Day 3, Day 4 → 456
2,654 ⎰ ⋮ ? days after
32

total number sold $\rightarrow 2,654 − 32 = 2,622$
number sold in 4 days $\rightarrow 456$
number sold in 1 day $\rightarrow 456 ÷ 4 = 114$
$2,622 ÷ 114 = 23$
He took 23 days to sell 2,622 hens.
$23 − 4 = 19$

Answer The farmer would be left with 32 hens **19 days** later.

Page 33 Skill Set 6-B: Draw a Diagram/Model
The following problems require a different type of model from the ones before.
Example: A school has 2,000 students. Of those students, 350 join the Art Club and 450 join the Science Club. Of the remaining students, $\frac{1}{3}$ join the Computer Club, but the rest did not join any club. How many students did not join any club?

Think
• Use all of the data given to form the model.
• Work out the appropriate operations.
Solve

350	450	?
Art	Science	Computer

2,000

remaining →
$2,000 − 350 − 450 = 1,200$
Computer Club $\rightarrow \frac{1}{3} \times 1,200 = 400$
$1,200 − 400 = 800$
Answer There were **800 students** who did not join any club.

Page 35 Skill Set 7-A: Look for a Pattern
To look for a pattern among the data given in a problem, examine the variables to find the specific pattern.
Example: Shauna wrote some numbers on a piece of paper. The numbers were written in 4 rows: A, B, C, and D. In which row will Shauna find the number 50?
Think
• Identify the relationship among the numbers.
• The numbers in row D are all multiples of 4.
• Find the answer using the information in row D.

A	1	5	9	13	17
B	2	6	10	14	18
C	3	7	11	15	19	23
D	4	8	12	16	20	2...

Solve

| D | 4 | 8 | 12 | 16 | 20 | 24 | 28 | 32 | 36 | 40 | 44 | 48 | 52 |

↑ 50 is before 52.

Work upward

A	...	49
B	...	50
C	...	51
D	...	52

Answer Shauna will find the number 50 in **row B**.

Page 38 Skill Set 7-B: Look for a Pattern
You can also look for a pattern and solve for letters and numbers arranged in certain positions.
Example: Grace writes some letters in the following pattern:

A   B   C   A   B   C   . . .   ?
1st 2nd 3rd 4th 5th 6th   16th

Which letter is in the 16th position?
Think
• Identify the relationship among the letters.
• The letters repeat after every 3 letters.
• Find the answer using multiples of 3.
Solve
In the 3rd and 6th positions, the letter is C. Since 3, 6, 9, and 15 are all multiples of 3, and since 16 is 1 after 15, the letter in the 16th position is A.
Answer The letter in the 16th position is **A**.

Page 40 Skill Set 8-A: Make a List/Table
Making a list or a table of the information given in a problem helps organize the data. This makes it easier to see missing data or recognize patterns.
Example: How many total numbers are multiples of 4 and less than 60?
Think
List all of the multiples of 4 that are less than 60.
Solve
Multiples of 4 $\rightarrow$ 4, 8, 12, 16, 20, 24, 28, 32, 36, 40, 44, 48,
52, 56, 60, . . .
↑
do not include 60

Answer There are **14 total numbers** that are multiples of 4 and less than 60.

Page 42 Skill Set 8-B: Make a List/Table
The following problems involve making a table and solving for connected numbers.
Example: Natalie rides her bike from town A to town B. She rides 12 kilometers on the first day, 10 kilometers the second day, 8 kilometers the third day, and so on. If the distance between the two towns is 40 kilometers, how long will Natalie take to reach town B?
Think
Make a table using the given information.
Solve

Day	1	2	3	4	5
Distance	12 km	10 km	8 km	6 km	4 km
Total	12 km	22 km	30 km	36 km	40 km

Answer It will take Natalie **5 days** to reach town B.

Page 44 Skill Set 9: Guess and Check
Guess and Check involves making calculated guesses and deriving a solution from them. It is a popular heuristic skill that is often used for upper primary mathematical problems. Because the guesses at the solutions can be checked immediately, the answers are always correct.
Example: Eboni opens a book. The sum of the two facing page numbers is 97. What are the page numbers?
Think
• Data given: the sum of the 2 numbers is 97.
• The page numbers of a book are consecutive.
• Create a guess-and-check table.
• Make at least 3 guesses to find the answer.
Solve

Page Numbers	Sum	Check
44 and 45	89	✗
45 and 46	91	✗
46 and 47	93	✗
47 and 48	95	✗
48 and 49	97	✓

Answer The page numbers are **48** and **49**.

Skill Set 1-A: Analyzing Parts and Wholes

Analyzing parts and wholes is a basic and useful way of looking at a problem. To analyze parts and wholes is to recognize the parts and understand how they form the whole.

Example:

Last week, 26,000 students took tests. Of those students, 19,612 took a language arts test and 5,000 took a math test. Of the remaining students, 10 took a history test. The remaining students took a science test. How many students took a science test? Round your answer to the nearest thousand.

Think

- Whole: 26,000; Parts: 19,612; 5,000; 10 of the remaining students; ? remaining students
- Draw the model.
- Solve by using appropriate operations based on the model.
- Round your answer to the nearest thousand.

Solve

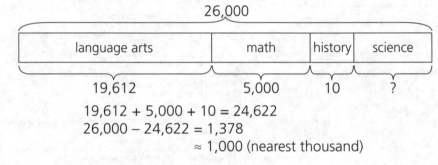

$$19,612 + 5,000 + 10 = 24,622$$
$$26,000 - 24,622 = 1,378$$
$$\approx 1,000 \text{ (nearest thousand)}$$

Answer About **1,000 students** took a science test.

Give it a try!

The Edwards family spent $13,000 on new furniture. They spent $8,800 on a sofa set and $3,480 on a dining table. They spent the remaining money on 2 identical chairs. How much money did they spend on each chair?

Think

Fill in the data. Solve by using appropriate operations based on the model.

Solve

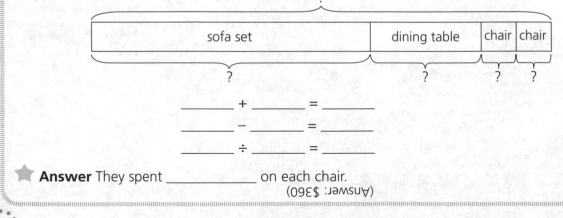

_____ + _____ = _____

_____ − _____ = _____

_____ ÷ _____ = _____

Answer They spent _____ on each chair.

(Answer: $360)

Practice: Analyzing Parts and Wholes

1. A shopkeeper had 4,985 pens and 16,207 pencils in her shop. She sold 2,680 pens and 7,986 pencils. She then threw away 16 faulty pens. How many total pens and pencils are left? Round your answer to the nearest hundred.

💡 **Think**

✏️ **Solve**

⭐ **Answer**

2. A desk costs $387, and a cupboard costs twice as much as the desk. Sam bought 1 desk and 2 cupboards. If he had $3,000, how much money does Sam have left?

💡 **Think**

✏️ **Solve**

⭐ **Answer**

Practice: Analyzing Parts and Wholes

3. A tailor bought 5 yards of cloth. He used $2\frac{3}{8}$ yards of cloth to make 1 pair of pants. If he made 2 pairs of pants, how much cloth does the tailor have left?

💡 **Think**

✏️ **Solve**

⭐ **Answer**

Skill Set 1-B: Analyzing Parts and Wholes

The previous problems asked you to solve for what was left. The next problems require you to find the total number of parts altogether, such as the whole, as well as each individual part.

Example:

Peter bought 14 rulers and three times as many erasers. How many rulers and erasers did he buy altogether?

💡 **Think**
- Parts: rulers → 14, erasers → 3 × rulers; Whole: total number of rulers and erasers
- Draw the model.
- Solve by using appropriate operations based on the model.

✏️ **Solve**

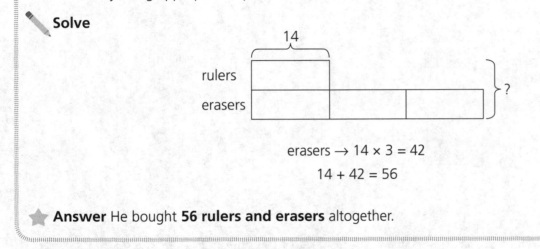

erasers → 14 × 3 = 42

14 + 42 = 56

⭐ **Answer** He bought **56 rulers and erasers** altogether.

Give it a try!

Mrs. Foster earns a weekly salary of $800. She saves $250, spends $370, and divides the remaining amount equally among her 3 children. How much does each child receive?

💡 **Think**
Fill in the data. Solve by using appropriate operations based on the model.

✏️ **Solve**

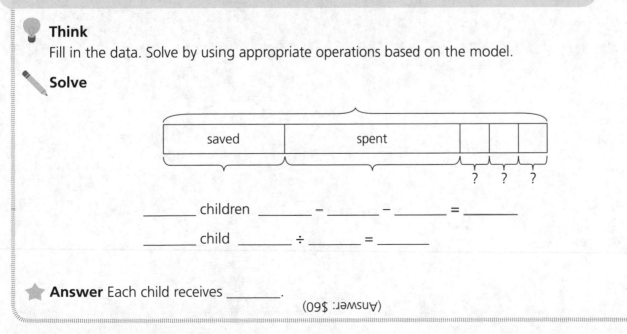

_____ children _____ – _____ – _____ = _____

_____ child _____ ÷ _____ = _____

⭐ **Answer** Each child receives _____ .

(Answer: $60)

4. A florist sold 24 red roses and twice as many pink roses on Saturday. He sold 36 pink roses and half as many red roses on Sunday. How many roses did the florist sell altogether?

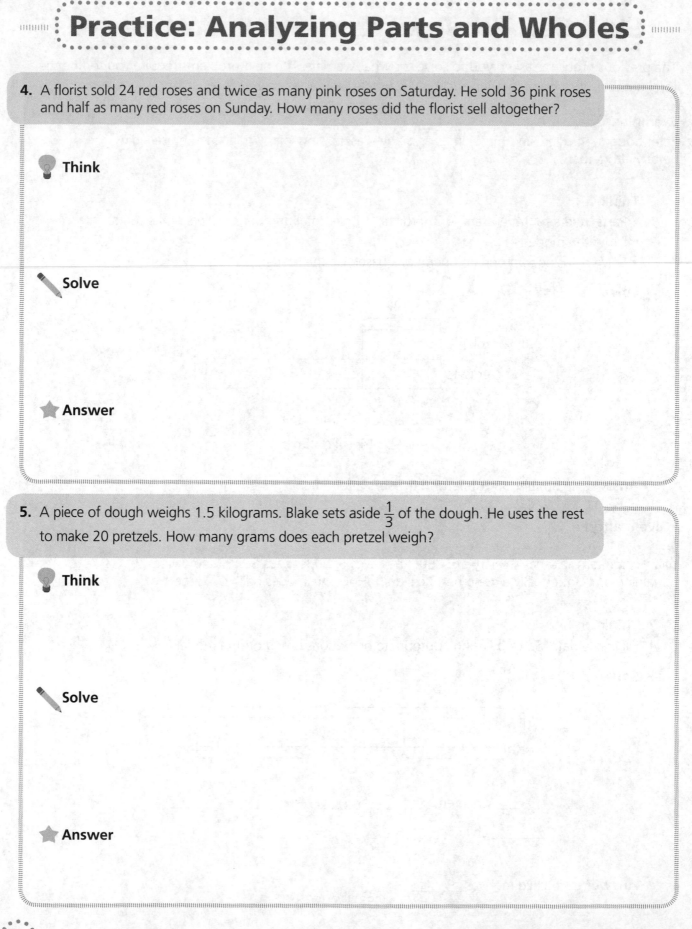

💡 **Think**

✏️ **Solve**

⭐ **Answer**

5. A piece of dough weighs 1.5 kilograms. Blake sets aside $\frac{1}{3}$ of the dough. He uses the rest to make 20 pretzels. How many grams does each pretzel weigh?

💡 **Think**

✏️ **Solve**

⭐ **Answer**

Skill Set 2: Comparing

Comparing is an effective way of identifying the relationship between the variables in a problem. Comparing the information in a problem helps you determine the differences in variables' quantities (for example, more or less).

Example:

Caitlin is 7 years older than her brother and 18 years younger than her aunt. In 2 years, her brother will be 9 years old. How old will Caitlin's aunt be in 15 years?

💡 **Think**

- Compare: Caitlin is 7 years older than her brother.
  Caitlin is 18 years younger than her aunt.
- Additional data: In 2 years, her brother will be 9 years old.
- Find the current ages first.
- Solve and find the answer.

✏️ **Solve**

Current ages:

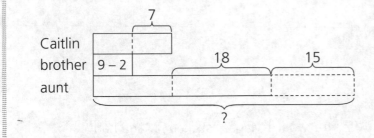

brother → 9 – 2 = 7 years old

Caitlin → 7 + 7 = 14 years old

aunt → 14 + 18 = 32 years old

In 15 years,

aunt → 32 + 15 = 47 years old

⭐ **Answer** Caitlin's aunt will be **47 years old** in 15 years.

Give it a try!

Ahmet is 26 years younger than his mother. In 4 years, his mother will be 3 times Ahmet's age. How old is Ahmet now?

💡 **Think**

Fill in the data and find the answer.

✏️ **Solve**

4 years later:

| Ahmet | |
| mother | |

_____ units → _____

1 unit → _____ ÷ _____ = _____

Now:

_____ – _____ = _____

⭐ **Answer** Ahmet is _____ **years old** now.

(Answer: 9)

Practice: Comparing

1. Tony, Davis, and Pedro went on a trip. Tony spent $1,924 more than Davis but $69 less than Pedro. If Tony spent $3,699, what was the total amount of money the three men spent on the trip?

💡 **Think**

✏️ **Solve**

⭐ **Answer**

2. Tracy and Maria had 45 stickers altogether. After Tracy gave Maria 5 stickers, Maria had 1 more sticker than Tracy. How many stickers did Tracy have to begin with?

💡 **Think**

✏️ **Solve**

⭐ **Answer**

3. Gabe, Leo, and Janelle share $628. If Gabe has $34 less than Leo, and Leo has half as much as Janelle, how much money does each person get?

💡 **Think**

✏️ **Solve**

⭐ **Answer**

4. Philip collected 50 more stamps than Xia. Darrell collected 20 fewer stamps than Philip. If Xia collected 250 stamps, how many stamps did Philip and Darrell collect altogether?

💡 **Think**

✏️ **Solve**

⭐ **Answer**

5. Cindy buys 4 identical geometry sets and 3 identical calculators for $95. Each calculator costs five times as much as a geometry set. How much does each calculator cost?

💡 **Think**

✏️ **Solve**

⭐ **Answer**

Skill Set 3: Identifying Patterns and Relationships

In number and pattern sequences, a relationship often exists among the data in the given arrangement. Always check the number or pattern sequence using the four operations, +, −, ×, or ÷, or rotate the patterns to find the relationship among the data.

Example:

Ben used 6 cubes to build a structure with 3 levels, as shown. How many cubes would Ben need to make a 10-level structure?

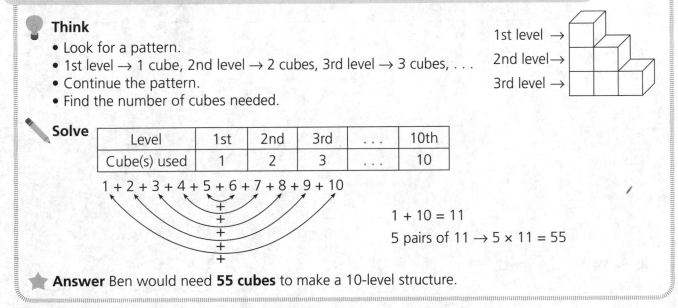

Think
- Look for a pattern.
- 1st level → 1 cube, 2nd level → 2 cubes, 3rd level → 3 cubes, . . .
- Continue the pattern.
- Find the number of cubes needed.

1st level →
2nd level→
3rd level →

Solve

Level	1st	2nd	3rd	. . .	10th
Cube(s) used	1	2	3	. . .	10

1 + 2 + 3 + 4 + 5 + 6 + 7 + 8 + 9 + 10

1 + 10 = 11
5 pairs of 11 → 5 × 11 = 55

⭐ **Answer** Ben would need **55 cubes** to make a 10-level structure.

Give it a try!

Ben uses 9 cubes to build a different structure with 3 levels, as shown. How many cubes will Ben need this time to make a 10-level structure?

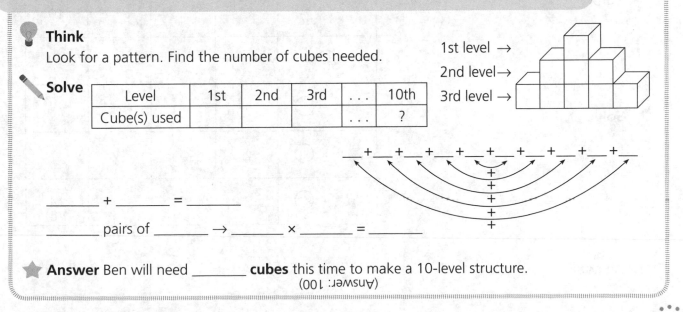

Think
Look for a pattern. Find the number of cubes needed.

1st level →
2nd level→
3rd level →

Solve

Level	1st	2nd	3rd	. . .	10th
Cube(s) used				. . .	?

_____ + _____ = _____

_____ pairs of _____ → _____ × _____ = _____

⭐ **Answer** Ben will need _____ **cubes** this time to make a 10-level structure.

(Answer: 100)

Practice: Identifying Patterns and Relationships

1. Study the pattern. Find the missing numbers.

| 2 | 6 | 3 | 9 | 3 | | 7 | | 4 | | 5 | | 8 |

💡 **Think**

✏️ **Solve**

⭐ **Answer**

2. Study the table. Find the missing numbers.

💡 **Think**

✏️ **Solve**

☆	2	4		10
◯	1		2	
☆ – ◯	1	2		
☆ × ◯	2		12	
☆ + ◯	3	6		14

⭐ **Answer**

Practice: Identifying Patterns and Relationships

3. Study the pattern. Find the missing numbers.

💡 **Think**

✏️ **Solve**

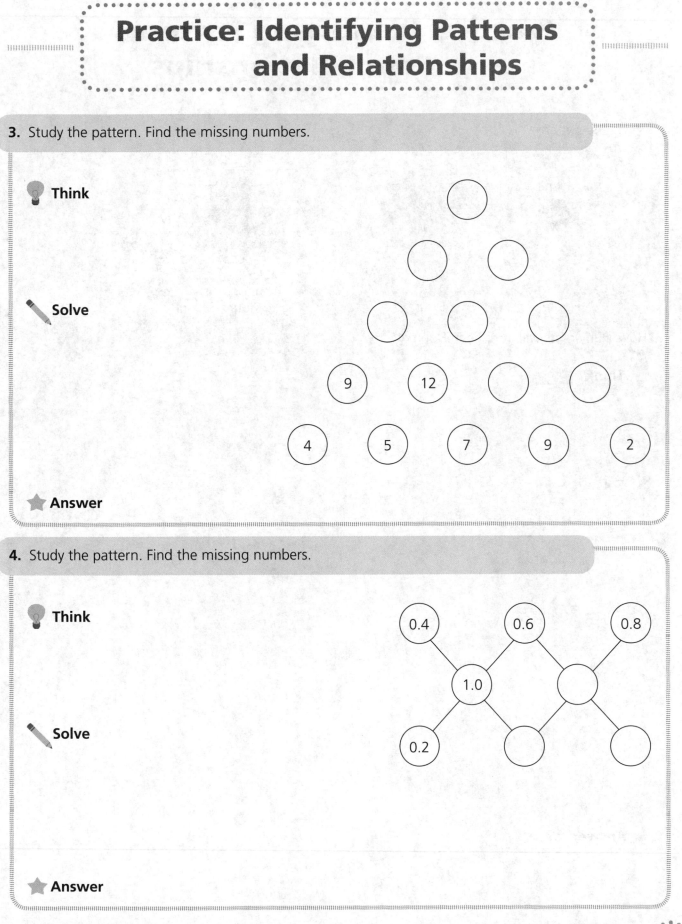

⭐ **Answer**

4. Study the pattern. Find the missing numbers.

💡 **Think**

✏️ **Solve**

⭐ **Answer**

Practice: Identifying Patterns and Relationships

5. Study the pattern.

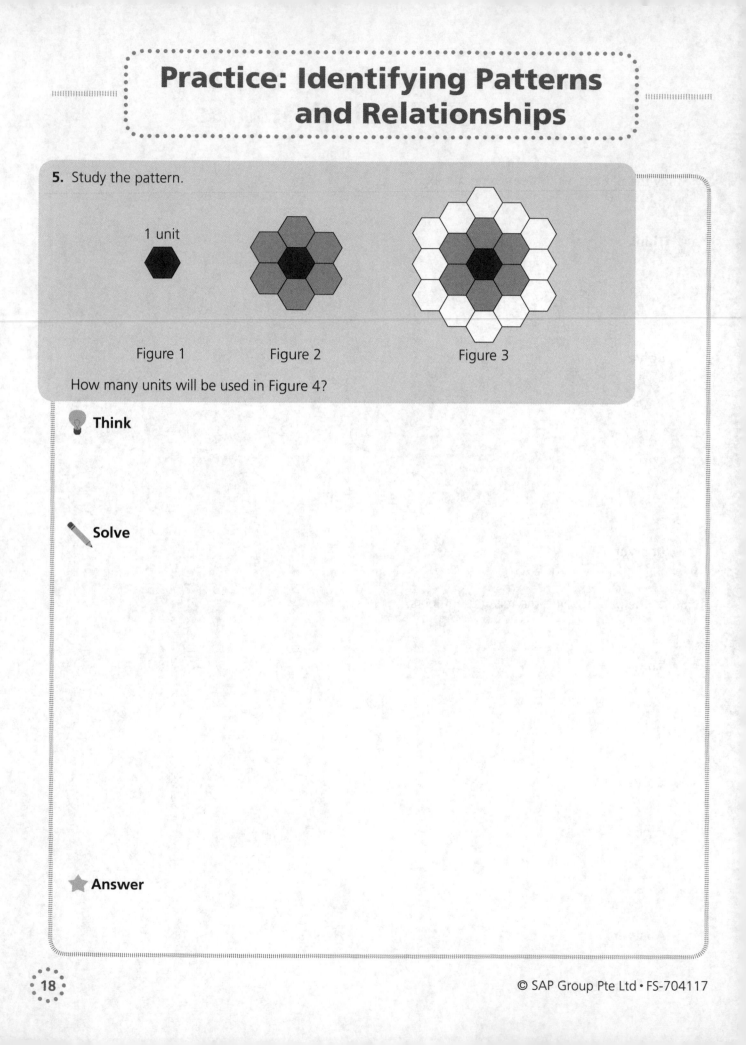

1 unit

Figure 1　　　　Figure 2　　　　Figure 3

How many units will be used in Figure 4?

💡 **Think**

✏️ **Solve**

⭐ **Answer**

Skill Set 4-A: Deduction

Deduction is a higher-order thinking skill that requires you to infer repeated computations from a given generalization. The information derived from the generalization will lead to a specific answer.

Example:

Study the figures. Fill in the table.

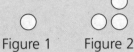

Figure 1   Figure 2   Figure 3

Figure	Pattern	Number of Circles
1	1	1
2	1 + 2	3
3		
4		
⋮	⋮	⋮
10		

Think

- Study the given information.
- Deduce the pattern from the given information and fill in the numbers.

Answer

Figure	Pattern	Number of Circles
1	1	1
2	1 + 2	3
3	**1 + 2 + 3**	**6**
4	**1 + 2 + 3 + 4**	**10**
⋮	⋮	⋮
10	**1 + 2 + 3 + 4 + 5 + 6 + 7 + 8 + 9 + 10**	**55**

Skill Set 4-A: Deduction

Give it a try!

Study the figures. Fill in the table.

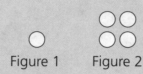

Figure 1   Figure 2   Figure 3

Figure	Pattern	Number of Circles
1		
2		
3		
4		
⋮	⋮	⋮
10		

Think

- Study the given information.
- Deduce the pattern from the given information and fill in the numbers.

Answer

Figure	Pattern	Number of Circles
1	___ × ___	
2	___ × ___	
3	___ × ___	
4	___ × ___	
⋮	⋮	⋮
10	___ × ___	

Answer:

Figure	Pattern	Number of Circles
1	1 × 1	1
2	2 × 2	4
3	3 × 3	9
4	4 × 4	16
⋮	⋮	⋮
10	10 × 10	100

Practice: Deduction

1. Study the figures. Draw Figure 4 and fill in the table.

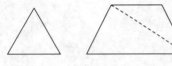

| Figure 1 | Figure 2 | Figure 3 | Figure 4 |

Figure	Number of Sides	Number of Triangles
1	3	1
2	4	2
3	5	3
4		
5		
⋮	⋮	⋮
10		

💡 **Think**

⭐ **Answer**

Practice: Deduction

2. Study the figures. Draw Figure 4 and fill in the table.

Figure 1   Figure 2   Figure 3   Figure 4

Figure	Number of Dots
1	3
2	3 + 3 = 6
3	3 + 3 + 3 = 9
4	
⋮	⋮
10	

💡 **Think**

🖍 **Solve**

⭐ **Answer**

Skill Set 4-B: Deduction

Besides applying deduction to shapes and figures, you can also use it to solve for missing numbers or representative letters and symbols in a grid.

Example:
Study the number grid. Find the value of the star.

💡 Think
- Study the given information.
- Deduce a pattern from the given information and find the value of the star.

1	2	3
13	*	5
21	34	55

✏️ Solve

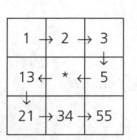

$1 + 2 = 3$
$2 + 3 = 5$
$3 + 5 = \mathbf{8}$
$5 + \mathbf{8} = 13$
$\mathbf{8} + 13 = 21$
$13 + 21 = 34$
$21 + 34 = 55$

⭐ **Answer** The value of the star is **8**.

Give it a try!

Study the grid. Find the values of X, Y, and Z.

💡 Think
Deduce a pattern from the given information and find the values of X, Y, and Z.

1	16	X
2	11	Y
4	7	Z

✏️ Solve

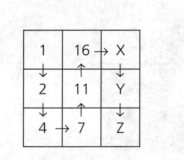

_____ + _____ = 2

_____ + _____ = 4

_____ + _____ = 7

_____ + _____ = 11

_____ + _____ = 16

X = _____ + _____

Y = _____ + _____

Z = _____ + _____

⭐ **Answer** X = _____, Y = _____, and Z = _____

(Answers: 22, 29, 37)

3. Study the number grid.

3	4	5
8	9	10
13	14	15

A. Now, study the following number grid. Find the missing number.

1	2	3
6	?	8
11	12	13

B. Using what you have deduced from part A, find the missing number in this number grid.

		29
	?	
37		

4. Study the letter grid. Find the missing letters by assigning number values to them.

A	G	C
D	I	
	B	H

💡 **Think**

✏️ **Solve**

⭐ **Answer**

Skill Set 5: Work Backward

Working backward is a strategy that uses a problem's final answer to find what the problem begins with. Very often, you can trace back the steps and reverse the operations to find the answers.

Example:

Think of a number. Double it. Add 8 to the result to get 22. What is the original number?

 Think

• Final answer: 22
• Reverse the operations to find the answer.

✏️ **Solve**

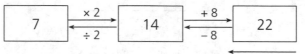

$$22 - 8 = 14$$
$$14 \div 2 = 7$$

⭐ **Answer** The original number is **7**.

Give it a try!

Think of another number. Divide it by 3 and add 5 to the result. Multiply the new result by 7 to get 56. What is the original number?

💡 **Think**

Reverse the operations to find the answer.

✏️ **Solve**

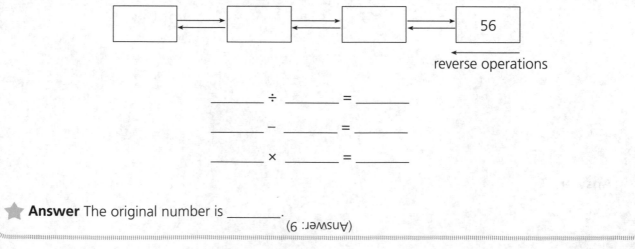

reverse operations

_____ ÷ _____ = _____

_____ − _____ = _____

_____ × _____ = _____

⭐ **Answer** The original number is _____.

(Answer: 9)

Practice: Work Backward

1. Fill in the missing numbers.

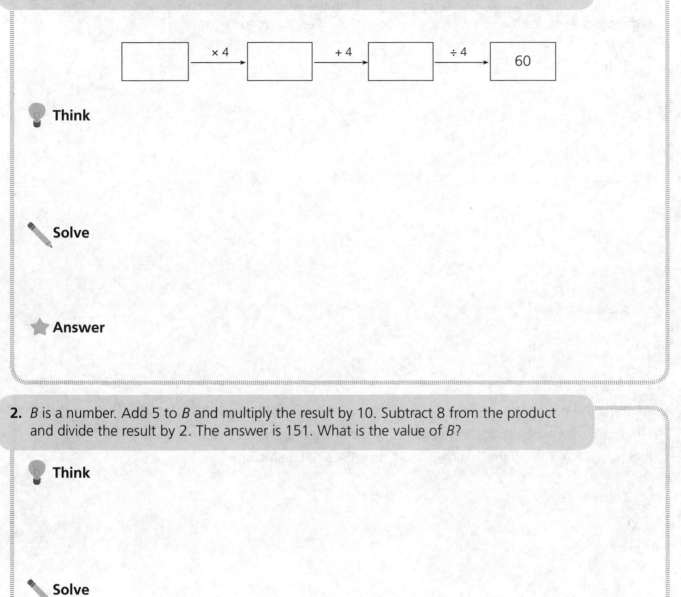

| | ×4 | | +4 | | ÷4 | 60 |

💡 **Think**

✏️ **Solve**

⭐ **Answer**

2. *B* is a number. Add 5 to *B* and multiply the result by 10. Subtract 8 from the product and divide the result by 2. The answer is 151. What is the value of *B*?

💡 **Think**

✏️ **Solve**

⭐ **Answer**

Practice: Work Backward

3. Together, bag A and bag B contain 100 marbles. Alicia removes 24 marbles from bag A and transfers 15 marbles from bag A to bag B. In the end, bag A and bag B have the same number of marbles. How many marbles were in each bag to begin with?

💡 **Think**

✏️ **Solve**

⭐ **Answer**

4. To prepare for a trip, Keisha spent $\frac{1}{4}$ of her money on clothes. She spent $\frac{1}{3}$ of the remaining money on a bag. She then bought a camera that cost $15 more than the bag and had $95 left. How much money did Keisha have to begin with?

💡 **Think**

✏️ **Solve**

⭐ **Answer**

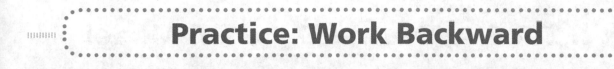

5. A train carrying some passengers left station A. At station B, 6 passengers boarded and 7 left. At station C, half of the passengers left the train. At station D, 5 passengers boarded and 8 left. As the train left station D, 28 passengers were on the train. How many passengers were on the train when it left station A?

💡 **Think**

✏️ **Solve**

⭐ **Answer**

Skill Set 6-A: Draw a Diagram/Model

Drawing diagrams or models helps you organize the data and identify the relationship among the data found in a problem. This skill set is similar to Analyzing Parts and Wholes, but it involves drawing a different type of model. Here, we will explore problem solving using multiplication and division models.

Example:

A farmer had 2,654 hens. He sold 456 hens in 4 days. If an equal number of hens were sold each day, how many days later would the farmer be left with 32 hens?

💡 **Think**

- Use all of the given data to form the model.
- Work out the appropriate operations.

✏️ **Solve**

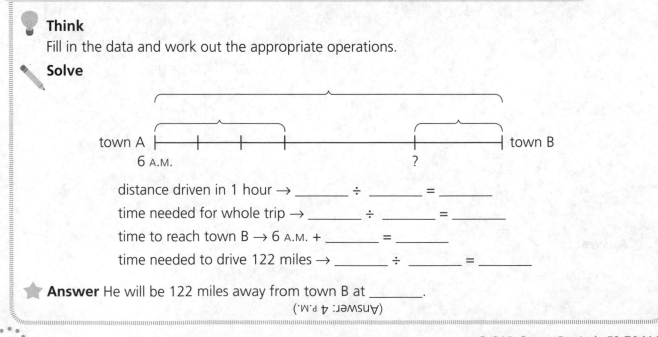

total number sold → 2,654 − 32 = 2,622
number sold in 4 days → 456
number sold in 1 day → 456 ÷ 4 = 114
2,622 ÷ 114 = 23
He took 23 days to sell 2,622 hens.
23 − 4 = 19

⭐ **Answer** The farmer would be left with 32 hens **19 days** later.

Give it a try!

Mr. Lang needs to drive from town A to town B, which are 732 miles apart. He leaves town A at 6.00 A.M. and drives 183 miles in 3 hours. If he drives the same speed throughout his trip, when will he be 122 miles away from town B?

💡 **Think**

Fill in the data and work out the appropriate operations.

✏️ **Solve**

town A |——+——+——+————————+—| town B
6 A.M.   ?

distance driven in 1 hour → _____ ÷ _____ = _____

time needed for whole trip → _____ ÷ _____ = _____

time to reach town B → 6 A.M. + _____ = _____

time needed to drive 122 miles → _____ ÷ _____ = _____

⭐ **Answer** He will be 122 miles away from town B at _____.

(Answer: 4 P.M.)

Practice: Draw a Diagram/Model

1. A book has 1,584 pages. Tisha reads an equal number of pages every day. But, she does not read on Sundays. How many pages must she read every day in order to finish reading the book in 3 weeks?

💡 **Think**

🖍 **Solve**

⭐ **Answer**

2. José and Colby had 1,152 marbles altogether. After José gave 29 marbles to Colby, Colby had three times as many marbles as José. How many more marbles did Colby have than José to begin with?

💡 **Think**

🖍 **Solve**

⭐ **Answer**

3. A school group went on a field trip to the zoo. The group had 6 times as many students as teachers. The group was made up of 602 people altogether. At lunchtime, each student ate 2 sandwiches, and each teacher ate 4 sandwiches. How many more sandwiches did the students eat than the teachers?

 Think

 Solve

⭐ **Answer**

The following problems require a different type of model from the ones before.

Example:
A school has 2,000 students. Of those students, 350 join the Art Club and 450 join the Science Club. Of the remaining students, $\frac{1}{3}$ join the Computer Club, but the rest did not join any club. How many students did not join any club?

Think
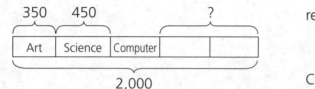
- Use all of the data given to form the model.
- Work out the appropriate operations.

Solve

350	450		?
Art	Science	Computer	

2,000

remaining →

$2{,}000 - 350 - 450 = 1{,}200$

Computer Club → $\frac{1}{3} \times 1{,}200 = 400$

$1{,}200 - 400 = 800$

Answer There were **800 students** who did not join any club.

Give it a try!

Chef Walsh has 2.4 kilograms of flour. He uses 75 grams for each of the 24 cookies he makes. How much flour does Chef Walsh have left?

Think
Fill in the data and work out the appropriate operations.

Solve

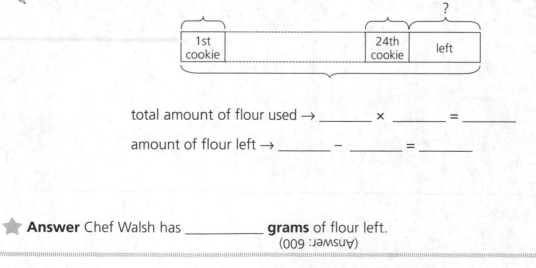

total amount of flour used → _____ × _____ = _____

amount of flour left → _____ – _____ = _____

Answer Chef Walsh has _____ **grams** of flour left.
(Answer: 600)

Practice: Draw a Diagram/Model

4. Melissa earns $1,620 a month. She spends $200 on transportation and $355 on food. She gives half of the remaining money to her mother. How much money does Melissa's mother receive from her each month?

💡 **Think**

✏️ **Solve**

⭐ **Answer**

5. Mr. Hansen ordered 3 batches of muffins, each weighing 6 pounds. He gave 18 ounces of muffins to each of his 12 relatives. How many ounces of muffins did Mr. Hansen have left? State your answer in pounds and ounces.

💡 **Think**

✏️ **Solve**

⭐ **Answer**

Skill Set 7-A: Look for a Pattern

To look for a pattern among the data given in a problem, examine the variables to find the specific pattern.

Example:

Shauna wrote some numbers on a piece of paper. The numbers were written in 4 rows: A, B, C, and D. In which row will Shauna find the number 50?

Think

- Identify the relationship among the numbers.
- The numbers in row D are all multiples of 4.
- Find the answer using the information in row D.

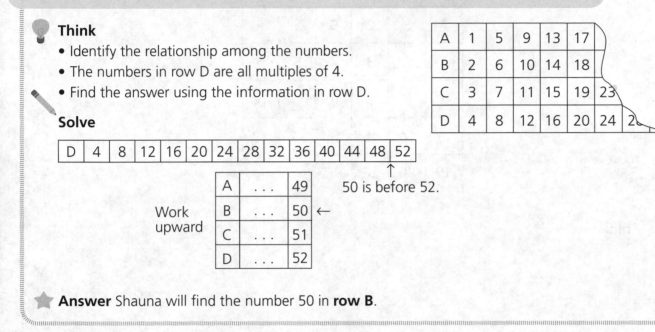

A	1	5	9	13	17		
B	2	6	10	14	18		
C	3	7	11	15	19	23	
D	4	8	12	16	20	24	2

Solve

| D | 4 | 8 | 12 | 16 | 20 | 24 | 28 | 32 | 36 | 40 | 44 | 48 | 52 |

50 is before 52.

Work upward	A	. . .	49
	B	. . .	50 ←
	C	. . .	51
	D	. . .	52

Answer Shauna will find the number 50 in **row B**.

Give it a try!

Shauna wrote some numbers on another piece of paper. This time, the numbers were written in 5 rows: A, B, C, D, and E. In which row will Shauna find the number 68?

Think

Find the answer using the information in row E.

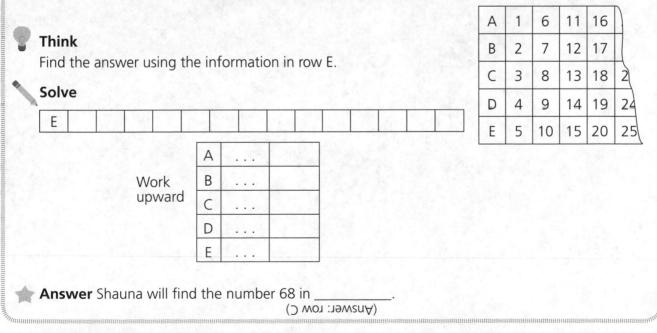

A	1	6	11	16	
B	2	7	12	17	
C	3	8	13	18	2
D	4	9	14	19	24
E	5	10	15	20	25

Solve

| E | | | | | | | | | | | | | | | | | | | | | |

Work upward	A	. . .	
	B	. . .	
	C	. . .	
	D	. . .	
	E	. . .	

Answer Shauna will find the number 68 in _____.

(Answer: row C)

Practice: Look for a Pattern

1. Chloe's teacher wrote numbers on a piece of paper in 6 columns: A, B, C, D, E, and F. But, he tore the paper and Chloe could not see some numbers. In which column will Chloe find 39?

A	B	C	D	E	F
1	2	3	4	5	6
7	8	9	10	11	12
13	14	15	16	17	18
19	20	21			

Think

Solve

Answer

Practice: Look for a Pattern

2. A factory used 4 liters of water on Monday, 6 liters of water on Tuesday, 10 liters of water on Wednesday, 16 liters of water on Thursday, and so on. How much water did the factory use on Saturday?

💡 **Think**

✏️ **Solve**

⭐ **Answer**

3. Uma saved money every month. She saved $5 in January, $10 in February, $20 in March, and so on. How many months did it take Uma to save a total of $315?

💡 **Think**

✏️ **Solve**

⭐ **Answer**

Skill Set 7-B: Look for a Pattern

You can also look for a pattern and solve for letters and numbers arranged in certain positions.

Example:

Grace writes some letters in the following pattern:

A	B	C	A	B	C	. . .	?
1st	2nd	3rd	4th	5th	6th		16th

Which letter is in the 16th position?

💡 **Think**

- Identify the relationship among the letters.
- The letters repeat after every 3 letters.
- Find the answer using multiples of 3.

✏️ **Solve**

In the 3rd and 6th positions, the letter is *C*. Since 3, 6, 9, and 15 are all multiples of 3, and since 16 is 1 after 15, the letter in the 16th position is *A*.

⭐ **Answer** The letter in the 16th position is **A**.

Give it a try!

Study the number pattern.

1, 2, 3, 4, 1, 2, 3, 4, . . .

What is the 23rd number?

💡 **Think**

Find the answer using multiples of 4.

✏️ **Solve**

Multiples of 4 → _____, _____, _____, _____, _____, _____

Number	Position
1	
2	
3	
4	

⭐ **Answer** The 23rd number is _____.

(Answer: 3)

Practice: Look for a Pattern

4. Zoe wrote her name and formed the following pattern:

Z	O	E	Z	O	E	. . .	?
1st	2nd	3rd	4th	5th	6th		30th

Which letter is in the 30th position?

💡 **Think**

✏️ **Solve**

⭐ **Answer**

5. Study the number pattern.

4, 1, 5, 2, 4, 1, 5, 2, . . .

What is the 30th number?

💡 **Think**

✏️ **Solve**

⭐ **Answer**

Making a list or a table of the information given in a problem helps organize the data. This makes it easier to see missing data or recognize patterns.

Example:

How many total numbers are multiples of 4 and less than 60?

💡 **Think**

List all of the multiples of 4 that are less than 60.

✏️ **Solve**

Multiples of 4 → 4, 8, 12, 16, 20, 24, 28, 32, 36, 40, 44, 48, 52, 56, 60, . . .

↑

do not include 60

⭐ **Answer** There are **14 total numbers** that are multiples of 4 and less than 60.

Give it a try!

How many total numbers are multiples of 6 and less than 100?

💡 **Think**

List all of the multiples of 6 that are less than 100.

✏️ **Solve**

Multiples of 6 → _____, _____, _____, _____, _____, _____, _____, _____, _____, _____, _____, _____, _____, _____, _____, _____, . . .

⭐ **Answer** There are _____ **total numbers** that are multiples of 6 and less than 100.

(Answer: 16)

1. Mrs. Espinosa has more than 25 but fewer than 35 treats to give to her students. If she gives each student 3 treats, she will have no more treats left. If she gives each student 4 treats, she will be 10 treats short. How many treats does Mrs. Espinosa have?

💡 **Think**

✏️ **Solve**

⭐ **Answer**

2. Mr. Chung bought between 30 and 40 stickers. If he gives 5 stickers to each of his nieces, he will be 3 stickers short. If he gives 3 stickers to each of his nieces, he will be left with 11 stickers. How many stickers did Mr. Chung buy?

💡 **Think**

✏️ **Solve**

⭐ **Answer**

Skill Set 8-B: Make a List/Table

The following problems involve making a table and solving for connected numbers.

Example:

Natalie rides her bike from town A to town B. She rides 12 kilometers on the first day, 10 kilometers the second day, 8 kilometers the third day, and so on. If the distance between the two towns is 40 kilometers, how long will Natalie take to reach town B?

💡 **Think**

Make a table using the given information.

✏️ **Solve**

Day	1	2	3	4	5
Distance	12 km	10 km	8 km	6 km	4 km
Total	12 km	22 km	30 km	36 km	40 km

⭐ **Answer** It will take Natalie **5 days** to reach town B.

Challenge yourself!

3. Morgan reads a book. He reads 13 pages on the first day, 11 pages on the second day, 9 pages on the third day, and so on. If the book has 49 pages, how long will Morgan take to finish reading the book?

💡 **Think**

✏️ **Solve**

⭐ **Answer**

4. Last weekend, 28 tennis matches were played at a tennis tournament. If each player was allowed to play only once with each other player, how many players were there altogether?

💡 **Think**

✏️ **Solve**

⭐ **Answer**

Skill Set 9: Guess and Check

Guess and Check involves making calculated guesses and deriving a solution from them. It is a popular heuristic skill that is often used for upper primary mathematical problems. Because the guesses at the solutions can be checked immediately, the answers are always correct.

Example:

Eboni opens a book. The sum of the two facing page numbers is 97. What are the page numbers?

 Think

- Data given: the sum of the 2 numbers is 97.
- The page numbers of a book are consecutive.
- Create a guess-and-check table.
- Make at least 3 guesses to find the answer.

Solve

Page Numbers	Sum	Check
44 and 45	89	✗
45 and 46	91	✗
46 and 47	93	✗
47 and 48	95	✗
48 and 49	97	✓

⭐ **Answer** The page numbers are **48** and **49**.

Give it a try!

Britney is three years older than Amber. The product of their ages is 378. How old is each girl?

Think

Make at least 3 guesses to find the answer.

Solve

Ages	Product	Check

⭐ **Answer** Britney is _____ **years old**, and Amber is _____ **years old**.

(Answers: 21, 18)

Practice: Guess and Check

1. Terrance opens a book. The product of the two facing page numbers is 156. If the book has 40 pages, what are the two page numbers?

💡 **Think**

✏️ **Solve**

⭐ **Answer**

2. Yow has 23 coins. Some are 10¢ coins, and the rest are 25¢ coins. Yow has more 10¢ coins than 25¢ coins. The total value of the coins is $3.95. How many 10¢ coins does Yow have?

💡 **Think**

✏️ **Solve**

⭐ **Answer**

Practice: Guess and Check

3. Adam bought a total of 12 pens and pencils. The pens cost $2 each, and the pencils cost $1 each. If Adam spent a total of $20, how many pens did he buy?

💡 **Think**

✏️ **Solve**

⭐ **Answer**

4. A total of 16 bicycles and tricycles are at a park. They have 36 wheels altogether. How many bicycles are at the park?

💡 **Think**

✏️ **Solve**

⭐ **Answer**

5. Davetta has 24 pens and pencils altogether. If she exchanges every pen for 2 pencils, she would have a total of 34 pencils.

A. How many pens does Davetta have?

B. How many pencils does Davetta have?

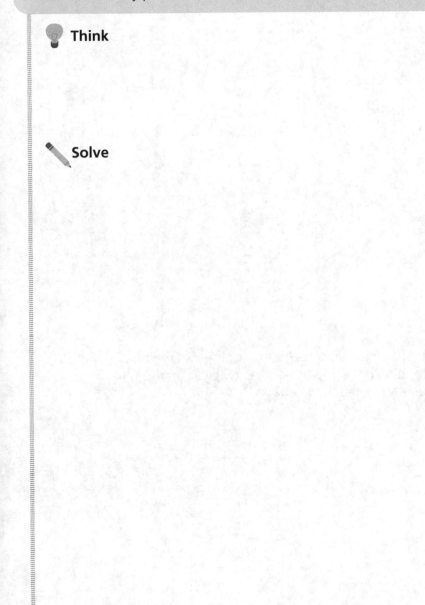

Think

Solve

Answer

Mixed Practice: Easy

1. Study the pattern. Find the missing numbers.

(9, 3), (36, 6), (16, 4), (☐ , 2), (81, ☐)

💡 **Think**

✏️ **Solve**

⭐ **Answer**

2. A golfer packs 500 golf balls into 4 bags. The first bag contains 142 golf balls. The third bag has 30 more golf balls than the second bag. The fourth bag has twice as many golf balls as the third bag. How many golf balls are in the third bag?

💡 **Think**

✏️ **Solve**

⭐ **Answer**

3. Mrs. Rivera mixed 4 liters of sugar water with $2\frac{4}{5}$ liters of lemon juice to make lemonade. While mixing, Mrs. Rivera spilled $\frac{1}{5}$ liter of lemonade. How many liters of lemonade are left?

💡 **Think**

✏️ **Solve**

⭐ **Answer**

4. Nicole had only $1 bills and $5 bills in her purse. If she had 27 bills altogether and a total of $71, how many $1 bills did Nicole have?

💡 **Think**

✏️ **Solve**

⭐ **Answer**

5. Fill in the boxes with the numbers 1 to 5 to complete the problem. Use each number only once.

💡 **Think**

+		

✏️ **Solve**

    5   6   4

⭐ **Answer**

6. Quan has 3 coins. The coins' sides are either "heads" or "tails." If Quan tosses the coins, how many different combinations of coin sides can he get?

💡 **Think**

✏️ **Solve**

⭐ **Answer**

7. Ivy, Dylan, and Abbie shared 100 stamps. Ivy received 8 more stamps than Dylan. Abbie received twice as many stamps as Ivy. How many stamps did each child receive?

💡 **Think**

✏️ **Solve**

⭐ **Answer**

8. Shay is 24 years old. Her brother is 3 years older than she is. In how many years will the sum of their ages be 59?

💡 **Think**

✏️ **Solve**

⭐ **Answer**

Mixed Practice: Intermediate

1. Container A and container B had 225 quarts of water altogether. Container A had 25 quarts more water than container B. Some water was poured from container A into container B so that container B had twice as much water as container A. How much water was poured from container A into container B?

💡 **Think**

✏️ **Solve**

⭐ **Answer**

2. The weight of 2 watermelons and 4 mangoes is the same as 4 papayas. How many papayas will weigh the same as 3 watermelons and 6 mangoes?

💡 **Think**

✏️ **Solve**

⭐ **Answer**

3. Kyle and Luke were putting together 2 similar puzzles. Luke took 4 minutes longer than Kyle to complete his puzzle. It took the two boys 26 minutes to complete the puzzles. If Luke's time was a multiple of 3, how long did Kyle take to complete his puzzle?

💡 **Think**

✏️ **Solve**

⭐ **Answer**

4. Every week, Delia's mom gave her a fixed allowance. On the week of her birthday, her mom gave her twice as much as the usual weekly allowance. In that week, Delia spent $10 and bought a book with half of the remaining money. She was left with $12. If there are 4 weeks in a month, what is Delia's usual monthly allowance?

💡 **Think**

✏️ **Solve**

⭐ **Answer**

5. Mr. Silva spent $160 on school supplies. A stapler cost $3 and a pair of scissors cost $1 more than a stapler. If he bought five times more pairs of scissors than staplers, how many pairs of scissors did Mr. Silva buy?

💡 **Think**

✏️ **Solve**

⭐ **Answer**

6. Renee has fewer than 50 cards but more than 20 cards. If she divides them into groups of 8, she will be 4 cards short. If she divides them into groups of 3, she will be left with 2 cards. How many cards does Renee have?

💡 **Think**

✏️ **Solve**

⭐ **Answer**

7. Study the pattern. Find the missing numbers.

| 2 | 4 | 6 | 6 | 8 | 14 | | | |

💡 **Think**

✏️ **Solve**

⭐ **Answer**

8. Drew had 320 picture cards. After giving 80 picture cards to Blane, he still had twice as many picture cards as Blane. How many picture cards did Blane have to begin with?

💡 **Think**

✏️ **Solve**

⭐ **Answer**

Mixed Practice: Challenging

1. Find the value of T.

P + Q = R
R + S = T
P + T = U
Q + S + U = 40

💡 **Think**

✏️ **Solve**

⭐ **Answer**

2. Mrs. Girard has to label 50 chairs from 1 to 50. What is the sum of the numbers on the last 20 chairs?

💡 **Think**

✏️ **Solve**

⭐ **Answer**

Mixed Practice: Challenging

3. Fill in the blanks with the numbers 2 through 7 to make a correct mathematical statement.

$$\boxed{} \times \boxed{} = \boxed{} \times \boxed{} = \boxed{} + \boxed{}$$

💡 **Think**

✏️ **Solve**

⭐ **Answer**

4. Each figure below represents a digit. The first three numbers, which may not be listed in order, are 835, 418, and 543. What number does D represent?

💡 **Think**

✏️ **Solve**

Letter	Number
A	◇ ☆ ○
B	○ □ ☆
C	□ ♡ ◇
D	♡ ◇ ○

⭐ **Answer**

5. Victor writes a string of letters in the following pattern:

A B B C C C A B B C C C . . .

If he continues the pattern and writes a total of 65 letters, how many B's are in the pattern altogether?

💡 **Think**

✏️ **Solve**

⭐ **Answer**

---

6. Study the pattern. Find the missing numbers.

2	3	4	2	3	4	5	7				

💡 **Think**

✏️ **Solve**

⭐ **Answer**

Answer Key

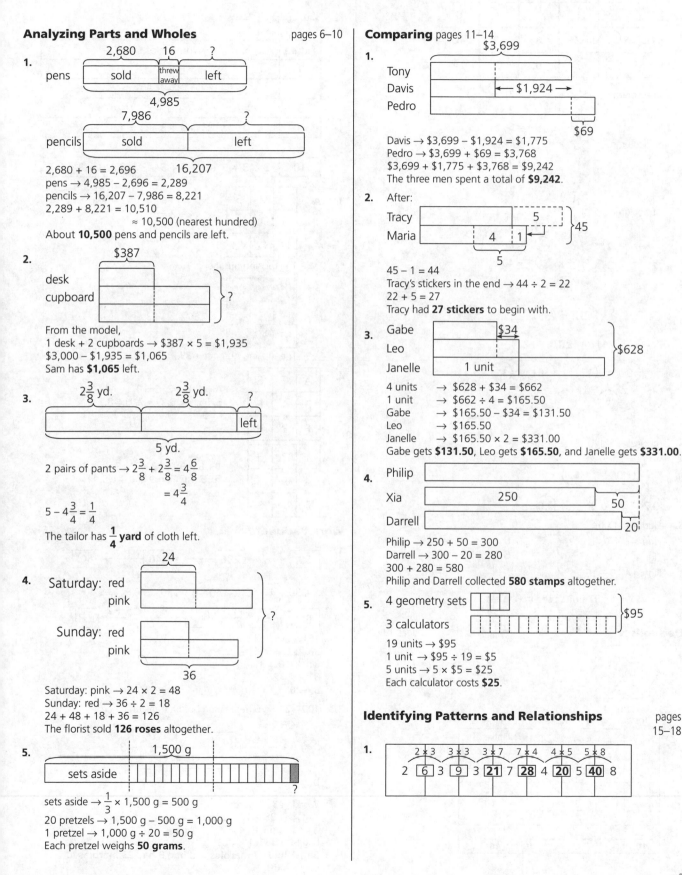

Analyzing Parts and Wholes
pages 6–10

1.

pens

2,680	16	?
sold	threw away	left

4,985

pencils

7,986	?
sold	left

16,207

2,680 + 16 = 2,696
pens → 4,985 – 2,696 = 2,289
pencils → 16,207 – 7,986 = 8,221
2,289 + 8,221 = 10,510
                    ≈ 10,500 (nearest hundred)
About **10,500** pens and pencils are left.

2.

$387

desk
cupboard   }?

From the model,
1 desk + 2 cupboards → $387 × 5 = $1,935
$3,000 – $1,935 = $1,065
Sam has **$1,065** left.

3.

$2\frac{3}{8}$ yd. $2\frac{3}{8}$ yd.   ?

left

5 yd.

2 pairs of pants → $2\frac{3}{8} + 2\frac{3}{8} = 4\frac{6}{8}$

$= 4\frac{3}{4}$

$5 - 4\frac{3}{4} = \frac{1}{4}$

The tailor has $\frac{1}{4}$ **yard** of cloth left.

4.

Saturday: red
             pink

24

Sunday: red
             pink

36   }?

Saturday: pink → 24 × 2 = 48
Sunday: red → 36 ÷ 2 = 18
24 + 48 + 18 + 36 = 126
The florist sold **126 roses** altogether.

5.

1,500 g

sets aside		

?

sets aside → $\frac{1}{3}$ × 1,500 g = 500 g

20 pretzels → 1,500 g – 500 g = 1,000 g
1 pretzel → 1,000 g ÷ 20 = 50 g
Each pretzel weighs **50 grams**.

Comparing
pages 11–14

1.

$3,699

Tony
Davis   ←—$1,924—→
Pedro

$69

Davis → $3,699 – $1,924 = $1,775
Pedro → $3,699 + $69 = $3,768
$3,699 + $1,775 + $3,768 = $9,242
The three men spent a total of **$9,242**.

2. After:

Tracy   5
                              }45
Maria   4   1

5

45 – 1 = 44
Tracy's stickers in the end → 44 ÷ 2 = 22
22 + 5 = 27
Tracy had **27 stickers** to begin with.

3.

Gabe $34
Leo
Janelle   1 unit   }$628

4 units   → $628 + $34 = $662
1 unit   → $662 ÷ 4 = $165.50
Gabe   → $165.50 – $34 = $131.50
Leo   → $165.50
Janelle   → $165.50 × 2 = $331.00
Gabe gets **$131.50**, Leo gets **$165.50**, and Janelle gets **$331.00**.

4.

Philip
Xia   250   50
Darrell   20

Philip → 250 + 50 = 300
Darrell → 300 – 20 = 280
300 + 280 = 580
Philip and Darrell collected **580 stamps** altogether.

5.

4 geometry sets

3 calculators   }$95

19 units → $95
1 unit → $95 ÷ 19 = $5
5 units → 5 × $5 = $25
Each calculator costs **$25**.

Identifying Patterns and Relationships
pages 15–18

1.

2	2×3	3	3×3	3	3×7	7	7×4	4	4×5	5	5×8	8
	6		**9**		**21**		**28**		**20**		**40**	

2.

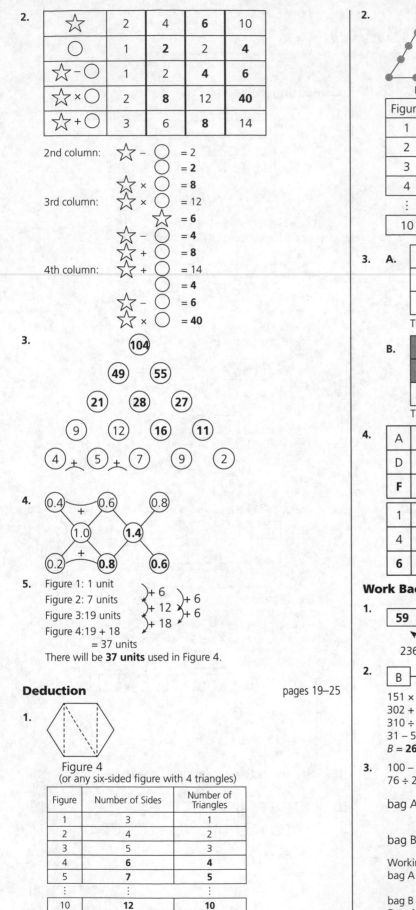

☆	2	4	**6**	10
○	1	**2**	2	**4**
☆ − ○	1	2	**4**	**6**
☆ × ○	2	**8**	12	**40**
☆ + ○	3	6	**8**	14

2nd column: ☆ − ○ = 2
○ = **2**
☆ × ○ = **8**

3rd column: ☆ × ○ = 12
☆ = **6**
☆ − ○ = **4**
☆ + ○ = **8**

4th column: ☆ + ○ = 14
○ = **4**
☆ − ○ = **6**
☆ × ○ = **40**

3.

(104)
(49) (55)
(21) (28) (27)
(9) (12) (**16**) (**11**)
(4) + (5) + (7) (9) (2)

4.

(0.4) + (0.6) (0.8)
(1.0) (**1.4**)
(0.2) + (**0.8**) (**0.6**)

5. Figure 1: 1 unit
Figure 2: 7 units ⎫ + 6 ⎫ + 6
Figure 3: 19 units ⎬ + 12 ⎬ + 6
Figure 4: 19 + 18 ⎭ + 18 ⎭
= 37 units
There will be **37 units** used in Figure 4.

Deduction
pages 19–25

1.

Figure 4
(or any six-sided figure with 4 triangles)

Figure	Number of Sides	Number of Triangles
1	3	1
2	4	2
3	5	3
4	**6**	**4**
5	**7**	**5**
⋮	⋮	⋮
10	**12**	**10**

2.

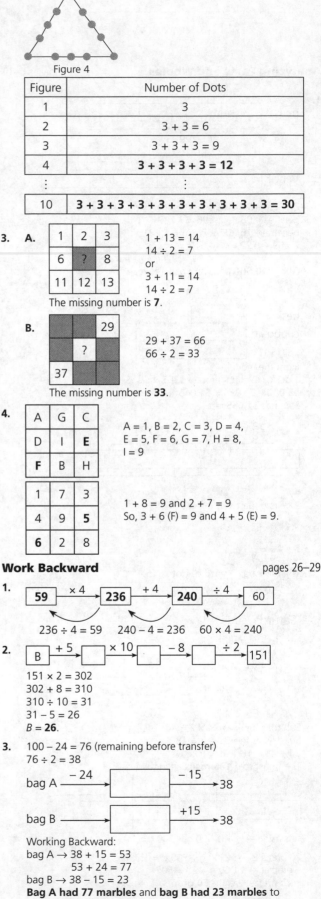

Figure 4

Figure	Number of Dots
1	3
2	3 + 3 = 6
3	3 + 3 + 3 = 9
4	**3 + 3 + 3 + 3 = 12**
⋮	⋮
10	**3 + 3 + 3 + 3 + 3 + 3 + 3 + 3 + 3 + 3 = 30**

3. **A.**

1	2	3
6	?	8
11	12	13

1 + 13 = 14
14 ÷ 2 = 7
or
3 + 11 = 14
14 ÷ 2 = 7
The missing number is **7**.

B.

		29
	?	
37		

29 + 37 = 66
66 ÷ 2 = 33
The missing number is **33**.

4.

A	G	C
D	I	**E**
F	B	H

A = 1, B = 2, C = 3, D = 4,
E = 5, F = 6, G = 7, H = 8,
I = 9

1	7	3
4	9	**5**
6	2	8

1 + 8 = 9 and 2 + 7 = 9
So, 3 + 6 (F) = 9 and 4 + 5 (E) = 9.

Work Backward
pages 26–29

1.

59 → × 4 → **236** → + 4 → **240** → ÷ 4 → 60

236 ÷ 4 = 59   240 − 4 = 236   60 × 4 = 240

2.

B → + 5 → ☐ → × 10 → ☐ → − 8 → ☐ → ÷ 2 → 151

151 × 2 = 302
302 + 8 = 310
310 ÷ 10 = 31
31 − 5 = 26
B = **26**.

3. 100 − 24 = 76 (remaining before transfer)
76 ÷ 2 = 38

bag A → − 24 → ☐ → − 15 → 38

bag B → ☐ → + 15 → 38

Working Backward:
bag A → 38 + 15 = 53
53 + 24 = 77
bag B → 38 − 15 = 23
Bag A had 77 marbles and **bag B had 23 marbles** to
begin with.

4.

$\frac{1}{4}$	$\frac{1}{4}$	$\frac{1}{4}$	$\frac{1}{4}$
clothes	bag	←camera→	left

Remaining → $\frac{3}{4}$

$15 $95

3 units → $\frac{3}{4}$

1 unit → $\frac{1}{4}$

1 unit → \$95 + \$15 = \$110
4 units → \$110 × 4 = \$440
Keisha had **\$440** to begin with.

5.

$$A \longrightarrow B \xrightarrow[-7]{+6} C \xrightarrow{\div 2} D \xrightarrow[-8]{+5} 28$$

28 − 5 + 8 = 31
31 × 2 = 62
62 − 6 + 7 = 63
The train had **63 passengers** when it left station A.

Draw a Diagram/Model
pages 30–34

1.

$$1{,}584 \begin{cases} \text{Day 1} \\ \text{Day 2} \\ \text{Day 3} \\ \vdots \\ \text{Day 18} \end{cases}$$

1 week → 6 days (minus Sunday)
3 weeks → 6 × 3 = 18 days
1,584 ÷ 18 = 88
She must read **88 pages** every day.

2. After:

Colby

José

} 1,152

4 units → 1,152
1 unit → 1,152 ÷ 4 = 288
Colby → 288 × 3 = 864
Before:

Colby |29|

José |29| ←

} 1,152

Colby → 864 − 29 = 835
José → 288 + 29 = 317
835 − 317 = 518
Colby had **518 more marbles** than José to begin with.

3.

students

teachers

} 602

7 units → 602
teachers → 1 unit → 602 ÷ 7 = 86
students → 6 units → 86 × 6 = 516
teachers' sandwiches → 86 × 4 = 344
students' sandwiches → 516 × 2 = 1,032
1,032 − 344 = 688
The students ate **688 more sandwiches** than the teachers.

4.

\$200	\$355	?	
transport	food	mother	Melissa

\$1,620

\$1,620 − \$200 − \$355 = \$1,065
\$1,065 ÷ 2 = \$532.50
Melissa's mother receives **\$532.50** from her each month.

5.

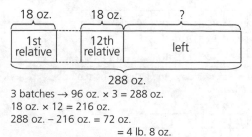

18 oz.	18 oz.	?
1st relative	12th relative	left

288 oz.

3 batches → 96 oz. × 3 = 288 oz.
18 oz. × 12 = 216 oz.
288 oz. − 216 oz. = 72 oz.
                    = 4 lb. 8 oz.
Mr. Hansen had **4 pounds 8 ounces** of muffins left.

Look for a Pattern
pages 35–39

1. F → multiples of 6
= 6, 12, 18, 24, 30, 36, 42

39 is before 42 ↑

A	B	C	D	E	F
⋮	⋮	⋮	⋮	⋮	⋮
37	38	39	40	41	42

↑

Chloe will find 39 in **column C**.

2.

	+2	+4	+6	+8	+10

Amount	4 L	6 L	10 L	16 L	24 L	34 L
Day	Mon.	Tues.	Wed.	Thurs.	Fri.	Sat.

The factory used **34 liters** of water on Saturday.

3.

	×2	×2	×2	×2	×2

\$	5	10	20	40	80	160
Month	Jan.	Feb.	Mar.	Apr.	May	June
Total \$	5	15	35	75	155	315

It took Uma **6 months** to save a total of \$315.

4. In every 3rd, 6th, 9th position, and so on, the letter is *E*. Since 3, 6, 9, and 30 are all multiples of 3, the letter in the 30th position is also **E**.

5. The repeated pattern has 4 numbers: 4, 1, 5 and 2.
4th position → 2
Multiples of 4 → 4, 8, 12, 16, 20, 24, 28, 32

↑
30 is before 32

30th	31st	32nd
1	5	2

The 30th number is **1**.

Make a List/Table
pages 40–43

1. Multiples of 3: . . ., 27, ⃝30, 33, . . .
Multiples of 4: . . ., 16, ⃝20, 24, . . .
10 treats short → difference = 10
                    30 − 20 = 10
Mrs. Espinosa has **30 treats**.

2. Multiples of 5: . . ., 30, 35, 40, . . .
        3 short: . . ., 27, ⃝32, 37, . . .
Multiples of 3: . . ., 18, 21, 24, . . .
        11 left: . . ., 29, ⃝32, 35, . . .
Mr. Chung bought **32 stickers**.

3.

Day	1	2	3	4	5	6	7
Pages	13	11	9	7	5	3	1
Total	13	24	33	40	45	48	49

Morgan will take **7 days** to finish reading the book.

4. Make a table:

• game played

	A	B	C	D	E	F	G	H	
A		•	•	•	•	•	•	•	7
B			•	•	•	•	•	•	6
C				•	•	•	•	•	5
D					•	•	•	•	4
E						•	•	•	3
F							•	•	2
G								•	1
H									

7 + 6 + 5 + 4 + 3 + 2 + 1 = 28

player A to H = 8 players

There were **8 players**.

Guess and Check pages 44–47

1.

Page Numbers	Product	Check
8 and 9	72	✗
9 and 10	90	✗
10 and 11	110	✗
11 and 12	132	✗
12 and 13	156	✓

The two page numbers are **12 and 13**.

2.

10¢ coins	Value	25¢ coins	Value	Sum	Check
14	$1.40	9	$2.25	$3.65	✗
13	$1.30	10	$2.50	$3.80	✗
12	$1.20	11	$2.75	$3.95	✓

Yow has **12 10¢ coins**.

3.

Pens	Value	Pencils	Value	Total Value	Check
6	$12	6	$6	$18	✗
7	$14	5	$5	$19	✗
8	$16	4	$4	$20	✓

He bought **8 pens**.

4.

Number of Bicycles	Number of Wheels	Number of Tricycles	Number of Wheels	Total Number of Wheels	Check
8	16	8	24	40	✗
9	18	7	21	39	✗
10	20	6	18	38	✗
11	22	5	15	37	✗
12	24	4	12	36	✓

There are **12 bicycles** at the park.

5.

Pencils	Pens →	2 pencils	Total number of pencils	Check
12	12 →	24	36	✗
13	11 →	22	35	✗
14	10 →	20	34	✓

A. Davetta has **10 pens**.
B. Davetta has **14 pencils**.

Mixed Practice: Easy pages 48–51

1. (9, 3) (36, 6) (16, 4) (⟦4⟧, 2) (81, ⟦9⟧)
  ↑ ↓ ↑ ↓ ↑ ↓ ↑ ↓ ↑ ↓
  3 × 3   6 × 6   4 × 4   2 × 2   9 × 9

2.
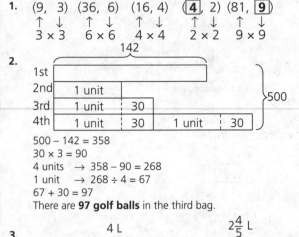

500 − 142 = 358
30 × 3 = 90
4 units → 358 − 90 = 268
1 unit → 268 ÷ 4 = 67
67 + 30 = 97
There are **97 golf balls** in the third bag.

3.
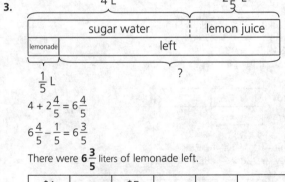

$\frac{1}{5}$ L

$4 + 2\frac{4}{5} = 6\frac{4}{5}$

$6\frac{4}{5} - \frac{1}{5} = 6\frac{3}{5}$

There were **$6\frac{3}{5}$** liters of lemonade left.

4.

$1 bills	Value	$5 bills	Value	Sum	Check
13	$13	14	$70	$83	✗
15	$15	12	$60	$65	✗
16	$16	11	$55	$71	✓

Nicole had **16 $1 bills**.

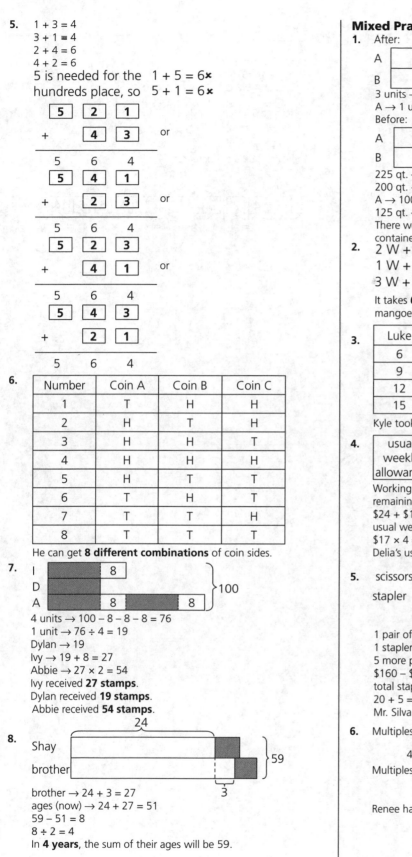

5.
1 + 3 = 4
3 + 1 = 4
2 + 4 = 6
4 + 2 = 6
5 is needed for the   1 + 5 = 6✗
hundreds place, so   5 + 1 = 6✗

| 5 | 2 | 1 |
+ | | 4 | 3 | or

| 5 | 6 | 4 |

| 5 | 4 | 1 |
+ | | 2 | 3 | or

| 5 | 6 | 4 |

| 5 | 2 | 3 |
+ | | 4 | 1 | or

| 5 | 6 | 4 |

| 5 | 4 | 3 |
+ | | 2 | 1 |

| 5 | 6 | 4 |

6.

Number	Coin A	Coin B	Coin C
1	T	H	H
2	H	T	H
3	H	H	T
4	H	H	H
5	H	T	T
6	T	H	T
7	T	T	H
8	T	T	T

He can get **8 different combinations** of coin sides.

7.
4 units → 100 – 8 – 8 – 8 = 76
1 unit → 76 ÷ 4 = 19
Dylan → 19
Ivy → 19 + 8 = 27
Abbie → 27 × 2 = 54
Ivy received **27 stamps**.
Dylan received **19 stamps**.
Abbie received **54 stamps**.

8.
brother → 24 + 3 = 27
ages (now) → 24 + 27 = 51
59 – 51 = 8
8 ÷ 2 = 4
In **4 years**, the sum of their ages will be 59.

Mixed Practice: Intermediate   pages 52–55

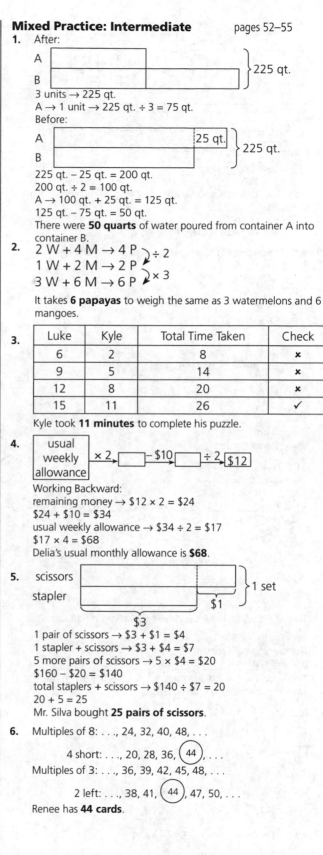

1. After:
3 units → 225 qt.
A → 1 unit → 225 qt. ÷ 3 = 75 qt.
Before:
225 qt. – 25 qt. = 200 qt.
200 qt. ÷ 2 = 100 qt.
A → 100 qt. + 25 qt. = 125 qt.
125 qt. – 75 qt. = 50 qt.
There were **50 quarts** of water poured from container A into container B.

2.
2 W + 4 M → 4 P ⟩ ÷ 2
1 W + 2 M → 2 P ⟩ × 3
3 W + 6 M → 6 P

It takes **6 papayas** to weigh the same as 3 watermelons and 6 mangoes.

3.

Luke	Kyle	Total Time Taken	Check
6	2	8	✗
9	5	14	✗
12	8	20	✗
15	11	26	✓

Kyle took **11 minutes** to complete his puzzle.

4.
Working Backward:
remaining money → $12 × 2 = $24
$24 + $10 = $34
usual weekly allowance → $34 ÷ 2 = $17
$17 × 4 = $68
Delia's usual monthly allowance is **$68**.

5.
1 pair of scissors → $3 + $1 = $4
1 stapler + scissors → $3 + $4 = $7
5 more pairs of scissors → 5 × $4 = $20
$160 – $20 = $140
total staplers + scissors → $140 ÷ 7 = 20
20 + 5 = 25
Mr. Silva bought **25 pairs of scissors**.

6. Multiples of 8: . . ., 24, 32, 40, 48, . . .

4 short: . . ., 20, 28, 36, (44), . . .
Multiples of 3: . . ., 36, 39, 42, 45, 48, . . .

2 left: . . ., 38, 41, (44), 47, 50, . . .
Renee has **44 cards**.

7.

multiples of 2

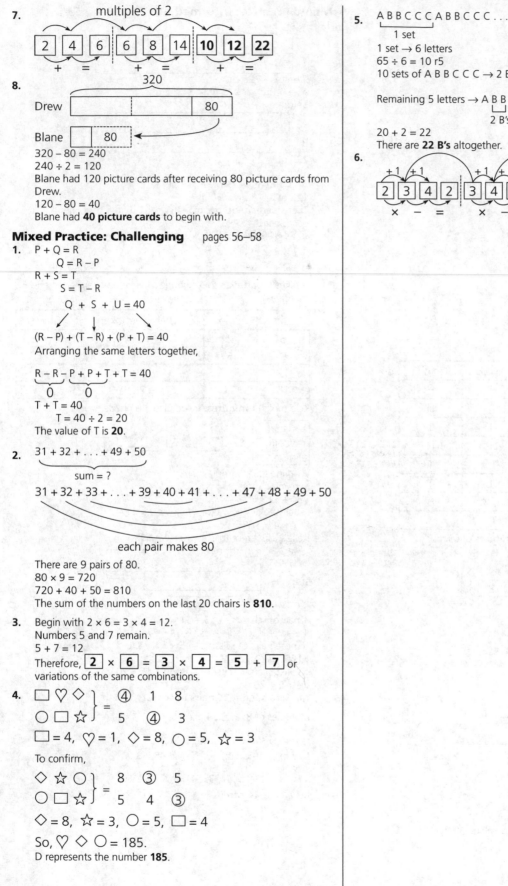

| 2 | 4 | 6 | 6 | 8 | 14 | **10** | **12** | **22** |

+ = + = + =

8.

320

Drew [| 80   ]

Blane [ ] 80 ←

320 − 80 = 240
240 ÷ 2 = 120
Blane had 120 picture cards after receiving 80 picture cards from Drew.
120 − 80 = 40
Blane had **40 picture cards** to begin with.

Mixed Practice: Challenging   pages 56–58

1.   P + Q = R
         Q = R − P
    R + S = T
         S = T − R
         Q + S + U = 40

(R − P) + (T − R) + (P + T) = 40
Arranging the same letters together,

R − R − P + P + T + T = 40
  0   0
T + T = 40
    T = 40 ÷ 2 = 20
The value of T is **20**.

2.   31 + 32 + . . . + 49 + 50

sum = ?

31 + 32 + 33 + . . . + 39 + 40 + 41 + . . . + 47 + 48 + 49 + 50

each pair makes 80

There are 9 pairs of 80.
80 × 9 = 720
720 + 40 + 50 = 810
The sum of the numbers on the last 20 chairs is **810**.

3.   Begin with 2 × 6 = 3 × 4 = 12.
Numbers 5 and 7 remain.
5 + 7 = 12
Therefore, [2] × [6] = [3] × [4] = [5] + [7] or variations of the same combinations.

4.   ☐ ♡ ◇ } = ④   1   8
    ○ ☐ ☆ }   5   ④   3

☐ = 4, ♡ = 1, ◇ = 8, ○ = 5, ☆ = 3

To confirm,

◇ ☆ ○ } = 8   ③   5
○ ☐ ☆ }   5   4   ③

◇ = 8, ☆ = 3, ○ = 5, ☐ = 4

So, ♡ ◇ ○ = 185.
D represents the number **185**.

5.   A B B C C C A B B C C C . . .
         └─────────┘
             1 set
1 set → 6 letters
65 ÷ 6 = 10 r5
10 sets of A B B C C C → 2 B's × 10 sets
                        = 20 B's
Remaining 5 letters → A B B C C
                       └──┘
                       2 B's
20 + 2 = 22
There are **22 B's** altogether.

6.

| 2 | 3 | 4 | 2 | 3 | 4 | 5 | 7 | **4** | **5** | **6** | **14** |

+1 +1   +1 +1   +1 +1
× − =   × − =   × − =